30 PROGRAMS FOR THE SINCLAIR ZX-80

* * *

1K

First published in the United Kingdom by
Melbourne House (Publishers) Ltd.

This remastered edition
published by
Acorn Books
www.acornbooks.co.uk

Copyright © 2020 Subvert Limited

All rights reserved. No part of this publication may be reproduced, stored in a retrieval system, or transmitted, in any form or by any means without the prior written permission of the publisher, nor be otherwise circulated in any form of binding or cover other than that in which it is published and without a similar condition being imposed on the subsequent purchaser. Any person who does so may be liable to criminal prosecution and civil claims for damages. All trademarks remain the property of their respective owners.

PLEASE NOTE
This book is a page-by-page reproduction of the original 1980 edition, one of the first books of this type ever published. The original was composed of pages mostly written on a standard typewriter, along with printed pages of code. As such, the quality of the text is rather different to that which might be expected of a more modern publication. The aim of this remastered edition however is to offer the reader as close an experience as possible to the original book; thus the original pages are presented with no changes, corrections nor updates. It should be noted that no guarantee is offered as to the accuracy of the information within.

Publisher's Note

We at Melbourne House are very excited to be involved with the publication of this book, making available as it does 30 interesting and varied programs for the SINCLAIR ZX 80, probably the first computer in the world to be readily accessible and affordable.

And we will not be stopping with the publication of this book - others are being prepared, including 'ZX-80 MACHINE LANGUAGE PROGRAMMING'.

We have a commitment to providing literature and software for the ZX-80, so if you have a program or an article which you think would be of interest to other ZX-80 users, please write to us.

We will give you a prompt assesment and reply whether the material is something we could use.

In the meantime, happy computing.

ALFRED MILGROM
PUBLISHER

Contents

Games to while the time away:

Leap Frog	1
Encoding	4
Horse Race	7
Lunar Lander	11
Mazes	15

Challenging the computer:

Noughts and Crosses	18
Dr. ZX 80	22
Nim	26
Blackjack	30

Playing with the computer:

Bubble sort	35
Line renumbering	37
Draw a picture	39
Machine code	44
Memory left	48

Computer shows off:

Day of the week	50

Chinese remainder   53
Simple simon   55

The computer as teacher:

Hangman   58
Maths drill   62
Capitals of the world   65
Life   69

Mathematical abilities:

Prime numbers   72
Simultaneous equations   74
Square root to 3 places   77

More games:

Bridge bidding   80
Pontoon   84
Chomp   88
Mastermind   91
Pinch   94

Pushing the computer limits:

Gomoku   98

Leap Frog

This is a nice simple program, testing the player's logic. The object is to move all the frogs on the left to the right, and vice versa. Frogs can only leap over one frog or move to an adjacent empty space.

```
● ● ● ●   0 0 0 0
1 2 3 4 5 6 7 8 9
```

The first move could be 35, 45, 65 or 75.

Variables: P   Position of frogs
             C   Number of moves to date
             F   "from"
             T   "to"

Program description:
    100 - 250   Initialisation
    300 - 370   Print routine
    500 - 620   Input player move
    700 - 760   Test if finished
    800 - 900   End

Leap Frogs

```
100 DIM P(9)
200 LET P(5) = 0
210 FOR I = 1 TO 4
220 LET P(I) = 129
230 LET P(I + 5) = 128
240 NEXT I
250 LET C = 0
300 CLS
310 FOR I = 1 TO 9
320 PRINT CHR$(P(I));" ";
330 NEXT I
340 PRINT
350 FOR I = 1 TO 9
360 PRINT I;" ";
370 NEXT I
500 PRINT "ENTER MOVE"
510 INPUT A
520 IF A = 0 THEN GO TO 900
530 LET F = A / 10
540 IF F = 0 THEN GO TO 510
550 IF P(F) = 0 THEN GO TO 510
560 LET T = A - 10 * F
570 IF T = 0 THEN GO TO 510
```

```
580 IF P(T) > 0 THEN GO TO 510
590 IF ABS(T - F) > 2 THEN GO TO 510
600 LET C = C + 1
610 LET P(T) = P(F)
620 LET P(F) = 0
700 LET X = 0
710 FOR I = 1 TO 9
720 IF I = 5 THEN GO TO 740
730 IF NOT P(I) = 128 - (I > 5) THEN LET X
    = 1
740 NEXT I
750 LET X = X + P(5)
760 IF X > 0 THEN GO TO 300
800 PRINT "YOU DID IT IN ";C;" MOVES"
810 PRINT "ANOTHER GO?"
820 INPUT A$
830 IF CODE (A$) = 62 THEN GO TO 200
900 PRINT "BYEBYE"
```

Encoding

An absolutely unbeatable method of producing secret messages! As the key to the coding is the ZX-80 random number generator, it would be impossible for anyone without a ZX-80 (and a lot of patience) to crack such a message.

To decode, just enter the negative of the code number that produced the message.

XJYF BZ TRDUBXA !

Variables: A$ message to be coded/decoded
                T   code number
                B   letter by letter value
                    coded / decoded

Program description:
   160   Sets coding key
   190 - 280   Coding / decoding

ENCODING

```
100 PRINT "ENTER MESSAGE"
110 INPUT A$
120 PRINT A$
130 PRINT "ENTER CODE NUMBER (1 - 256)"
140 INPUT T
150 PRINT T
160 RANDOMISE ABS(T)
170 IF T < 0 THEN PRINT "DE";
180 PRINT "CODED MESSAGE IS"
190 LET R = RND (26)
200 IF T < 0 THEN LET R = 26 - R
210 IF A$ = "" THEN GO TO 300
220 LET B = CODE (A$)
230 LET A$ = TL$ (A$)
240 IF B = 0 THEN GO TO 280
250 LET B = B + R - 38
260 LET B = B - 26 * (B / 26)
270 LET B = B + 38
280 PRINT CHR$ (B);
290 GO TO 190
300 PRINT
310 PRINT "ANY OTHER MESSAGE?"
320 INPUT A$
```

```
330 IF NOT CODE (A$) = 62 THEN GO TO 360
340 CLS
350 GO TO 100
360 PRINT "BYEBYE"
```

Horse Race

A day at the races without even having to leave the ZX-80! Four horses (A, B, C, and D) are assigned odds and you have £100 betting money.

Line 360 calculates how well the horse runs - the favourite is more predictable, but the long odds have more likelihood of being surprising.

This program is very full, especially when the race is being run as the screen display occupies a lot of memory.

The characters which make up the horses are (the shifted characters above the letters) A$: F,T,S. B$: (space),S,G,Q. C$: R,(space),(space),E.

Variables: M   Money left
              B   Bet
              O(I) Odds for each horse
              D, D(I) Distance covered

Horse Race

```
 50 RANDOMISE
 60 DIM O(4)
 70 DIM D(4)
 80 LET A$ = "..."
 90 LET B$ = "..."
100 LET C$ = "..."
110 LET M = 100
120 GO TO 200
130 FOR C = 1 TO D
140 PRINT " ";
150 NEXT C
160 RETURN
170 FOR I = 0 TO 4
180 LET D(I) = 0
190 NEXT I
200 PRINT "YOU HAVE £";M
210 PRINT "ENTER BET"
220 PRINT
230 PRINT "ODDS"
240 FOR I = 1 TO 4
250 LET O(I) = RND (9) + 1
260 PRINT CHR$ (I + 37), O(I); "/1"
270 NEXT I
280 INPUT B
```

```
290 IF B = 0 THEN GO TO 999
300 PRINT "HORSE?"
310 INPUT H$
320 FOR L = 1 TO 4
330 CLS
340 PRINT "LAP ";L
350 FOR I = 1 TO 4
360 LET D(I) = D(I) + 5 + 7 / O(I) + RND
    (2 * O(I) / 3)
370 IF D(I) > D(0) THEN LET D(0) = D(I)
380 IF D(0) = D(I) THEN LET J = I
390 NEXT I
400 FOR I = 1 TO 4
410 PRINT CHR$ (I + 37)
420 LET D = D(I) - D(0) + 15
430 GO SUB 130
440 PRINT A$
450 GO SUB 130
460 PRINT B$
470 GO SUB 130
480 PRINT C$
490 PRINT
500 NEXT I
510 PRINT "PRESS N/L"
520 INPUT D$
```

```
530 NEXT L
540 CLS
550 PRINT "WINNER IS "; CHR$ (J + 37)
560 LET S = 0
570 IF CODE (H$) = J + 37 THEN LET S = 1
580 LET M = M - B + S * B * O(J)
590 IF M < 1 THEN GO TO 999
600 GO TO 170
999 PRINT "BIBI"
```

Lunar Lander

A real live Lunar Lander that comes down to (hopefully) land safely on the Moon.

This program takes advantage of the fact that variables calculated or stored in a RUN are retained until they are CLEARed or another RUN is pressed.

By using the GO TO 100 instead, the Lunar Lander shape is retained in memory and the program lines which created it (200 - 250) are overwritten.

Variables: H,V,R   Height, Velocity, Fuel
            F,T   Thrust and duration
            A(I)   Lunar Lander shape
            L   Lines between Lander & the Moon

Program description:
    200 - 250   Lunar Lander shape then replaced by Print routine
    500 - 690   Display routine

NOTE: This program can be SAVEd, and the variables will also be saved.

Lunar Lander

```
 90 DIM A(19)
100 LET V = -50
110 LET H = 1500
120 LET R = 7000
200 FOR I = 0 TO 19
210 PRINT I,
220 INPUT X
230 LET A(I) = X
240 PRINT A(I)
250 NEXT I
```

> R*U*N
ENTER FOLLOWING VALUES:
0, 0, 156, 0, 0, 0, 8, 3, 136, 0, 0,
2, 3, 130, 0, 134, 131, 3, 131, 135

```
200 FOR I = 0 TO 3
210 FOR X = 0 TO 4
220 PRINT CHR$(A(X + 5 * I));
230 NEXT X
240 PRINT
250 NEXT I
```

> G*O T*O 1*0*0 TO VERIFY LUNAR LANDER SHAPE

```
130 GO TO 500
260 RETURN
300 PRINT "THRUST (0 - 99)?",
310 INPUT F
320 PRINT F
330 PRINT "DURATION (1-10)?",
340 INPUT T
350 CLS
360 IF F * T > R / 10 THEN LET F = R / 10 * T
370 LET R = R - F * T * 10
400 LET A = F - 32
410 LET H = A * T ** 2 + V * T + H
420 LET V = 2 * A * T + V
500 LET L = H / 100
510 IF L < 0 THEN LET L = 0
520 IF L > 12 THEN LET L = 12
530 FOR I = L TO 12
540 PRINT
550 NEXT I
560 IF L > 8 THEN GO SUB 200
570 PRINT , "VELOC","HEIGHT","FUEL"
580 PRINT , V, H, R
600 IF L < 9 THEN GO SUB 200
610 IF L = 0 THEN GO TO 650
```

```
620 FOR I = 1 TO L - 1
630 PRINT
640 NEXT I
650 IF H < 0 THEN PRINT "**CRASH**"
660 FOR I = 1 TO 16
670 PRINT "▰▱";
680 NEXT I
690 IF L > 0 THEN GO TO 300
700 IF H < 0 OR V < - 99 THEN GO TO 730
710 PRINT 100 + V;" PERCENT OK"
720 STOP
730 PRINT "TERRIBLE"
```

IMPORTANT NOTE:

TO RUN THIS PROGRAM, DO NOT PRESS R*U*N AS THIS WILL CLEAR THE VARIABLES WITH THE LUNAR LANDER SHAPE.
USE G*O T*O 1*0*0.

MAZES

A maze generating program: there are no guarantees that a solution is available, but it's unlikely you won't find one.

Slipping down the sides is considered cheating!

Each new line of the maze is dependent on the previous line, but no two runs will be the same.

Variables: W   32 characters of line

Program description:
    150 - 240   Creation of first line
    340 - 470   Creation of following lines

MAZES

```
100 DIM W(32)
110 PRINT
120 PRINT "IT/S AMAZING"
130 PRINT
140 LET W(1) = 2
150 LET W(32) = 130
160 FOR I = 2 TO 31
170 LET W(I) = 3
180 NEXT I
190 LET X = RND (20)
200 LET W(X) = 2
210 LET W(X + 6) = 130
220 FOR I = 2 TO 5
230 LET W(X + I) = 0
240 NEXT I
300 FOR L = 1 TO 15
310 FOR I = 1 TO 32
320 PRINT CHR$(W(I));
330 IF I = 1 OR I = 32 THEN GO TO 500
340 IF W(I) < 3 THEN GO TO 450
350 IF W(I) > 3 THEN GO TO 400
360 LET X = RND (8)
370 IF X < 3 THEN LET W(I) = 2
380 IF X = 8 THEN LET W(I) = 7
```

```
390 GO TO 500
400 LET W(I) = 1 + RND (2)
410 GO TO 500
450 LET X = RND (5)
460 LET W(I) = 1 + X / 2
470 IF X = 1 THEN LET W(I) = 7
500 NEXT I
510 NEXT L
```

Noughts And Crosses

The Computer challenges the world: Noughts and Crosses! (If you look at the program listing, there is only provision for the ZX 80 to win or for a draw.) Admittedly the computer always starts first.

This home ground advantage means that the program is always on the attack. The logic of the program may be difficult to follow from the listing but it is based on very simple rules.

Lines 110 - 180 are a 'force-feed' to generate the grid numbering system.

Variables: A   Grid
             M   Move
             P   Previous move
             R   Reply
             E   Denotes whether player's
                  first move was even.

Noughts and Crosses

```
100 DIM A(9)
110 FOR J = 0 TO 2
120 FOR I = 1 TO 3
130 LET A(I + 3 * J) = 28 + I + 4 * J +
    2 * I * (J > 1)
140 NEXT I
150 NEXT J
160 LET A(4) = 36
170 LET A(5) = 61
180 LET A(6) = 32
190 GO TO 400
200 FOR I = 1 TO 9
210 IF A(I) = M + 28 THEN LET A(I) = V
220 NEXT I
230 FOR I = 0 TO 2
240 FOR J = 1 TO 3
250 PRINT CHR$ (A(J + 3 * I));" ";
260 NEXT J
270 PRINT
280 PRINT
290 NEXT I
300 PRINT
310 RETURN
400 LET A = 0
```

```
410 LET E = 0
420 PRINT "I WENT FIRST"
430 GO SUB 230
440 PRINT "ENTER MOVE"
450 INPUT R
460 CLS
470 IF R = 2 * (R / 2) THEN LET E = -1
480 LET M = R
490 LET V = 28
500 GO SUB 200
510 LET P = R
520 FOR T = 1 TO 4
530 PRINT "I MOVED"
540 LET V = 61
550 LET A = A + 1
560 IF T = 1 OR R = P + 4 OR R = P - 4
    THEN GO TO 620
570 LET P = P + 4
580 IF P > 8 THEN LET P = P - 8
590 LET M = P
600 GO SUB 200
610 GO TO 790
620 IF A = 3 AND E THEN LET A = 7
630 IF A = 4 THEN LET A = 6
640 LET P = P + A
```

```
650 IF P > 8 THEN LET P = P - 8
660 LET M = P
670 GO SUB 200
680 IF A = 7 THEN GO TO 790
690 IF T = 4 THEN GO TO 770
700 PRINT "YOUR MOVE"
710 INPUT R
720 CLS
730 LET M = R
740 LET V = 28
750 GO SUB 200
760 NEXT T
770 PRINT "DRAW"
780 STOP
790 PRINT "ZX-80 WINS"
```

Dr. ZX-80

A computer analyst - and like some of his human counterparts, this one doesn't listen to a word you say.

The result can be quite amusing.

This program demonstrates how efficiently space can be organised, and a conversation generated that would probably otherwise strain the ZX 80 memory.

A$ contains all the words to be used, and once in the memory there is no need to also keep it in the program listing.

Each word is assigned a number (the number of bytes from the start of A$). It is therefore essential that A$ should be the first variable saved in the RUN, so that we can know where to PEEK.

This program can be SAVEd as with a normal program. Just remember not to press RUN, but to use GO TO 120 instead.

Dr. ZX-80

```
100 LET A$ = "A ACCEPTABLE AGAIN BYEBYE CO
    ME DID DO ENOUGH FEEL FIND FOR FRIENDS
     HELLO HERE HOW I IS I/M LIKE NAME NOR
    MAL REASONABLE SAY THAT/S THERAPIST TH
    ERE THINK THIS TO TODAY WAS WAY WHAT W
    HEN WHY WOULD YOU YOUR "
110 DIM P (90)
120 LET S = PEEK (16392) + 256 * PEEK (163
    93)
200 FOR I = 0 TO 90
210 PRINT I,
220 INPUT B
230 LET P(I) = B
240 PRINT P(I)
250 IF B = 0 THEN CLS
260 NEXT I
```

R*U*N
ENTER FOLLOWING VALUES:
68,141,88,199,131,175,85,199,97,0
175,32,195,120,199,97,167,14,0
79,36,195,46,161,0
36,195,147,153,85,109,0
185,36,195,147,195,46,153,171,0

23

36,199,60,51,153,3,0
36,195,27,74,158,51,60,0
36,195,147,153,85,102,0
36,199,60,51,153,3,0
83,147,124,39,56,161,180,189,195,92,158,
   27,74,14,0
124,109,20,0

CHECK THAT TABLE HAS BEEN ENTERED CORRECTLY
BY TYPING ON EDIT LINE (AFTER R*U*N ABOVE
BUT BEFORE ALTERING PROGRAM):
PRINT CHR$ (PEEK (S + 1)) - RESULT SHOULD
   BE 'A'
PRINT CHR$ (PEEK (S + 199)) - RESULT SHOULD
   BE 'Y'

NOTE: I STRONGLY RECOMMEND THAT YOU SAVE
THE PARTIAL PROGRAM AT THIS STAGE - IT WILL
SAVE YOU A LOT OF TEDIOUS RETYPING IF YOU
SHOULD LOSE THE PROGRAM SOMETIME AFTER THIS.

DELETE LINES 100 AND 110 AND REPLACE LINES
200 ONWARDS WITH FOLLOWING:

200 FOR I = 0 TO 88
210 LET J = -1
220 LET J = J + 1
230 IF P(I) = 0 THEN GO TO 270
240 PRINT CHR$ (PEEK (S + P(I) + J));
250 IF PEEK (S + P(I) + J) > 0 THEN GO TO 220
260 IF P(I) > 0 THEN GO TO 300
270 PRINT "?"
280 INPUT B$
290 CLS
300 NEXT I

IMPORTANT NOTE:

To run this program, do not press R*U*N as this will clear the variables.
Use G*O T*O 1*2*0.

NIM

NIM - the wonderful match game popularised by the movie 'Last Year at Marienbad'.

The object is take matches away in turn, but any player can remove matches from only one row at a time. From 1 to the number of matches in the row can be removed.

Rules vary, but the version here is that the player to take the last match wins.

The mathematical formula for winning is based on binary numbers: convert each row to binary, and add the rows in decimal fashion: e.g.

```
    7 matches   =   1 1 1
    2               0 1 0
    1               0 0 1
                    -------
                    1 2 2
```

A winning position is obtained if you can leave an even total in each column - e.g. removing 4 from row 1 in this case. The notation used in this program would be 14 (ie. Row 1, 4 matches).

NIM

```
100 DIM T(3)
110 DIM N(3)
120 DIM X(3)
130 LET N(1) = 7
140 LET N(2) = 5
150 LET N(3) = 3
160 GO TO 500
200 FOR R = 1 TO 3
210 FOR M = 1 TO N(R)
220 IF N(R) = 0 THEN GO TO 250
230 PRINT " ▓";
240 NEXT M
250 PRINT
260 PRINT
270 NEXT R
280 RETURN
300 FOR S = 0 TO 3
310 LET T(S) = 0
320 NEXT S
330 FOR S = 1 TO 3
340 LET T(1) = T(1) + (X(S) AND 4)/4
350 LET T(2) = T(2) + (X(S) AND 2)/2
360 LET T(3) = T(3) + (X(S) AND 1)
370 NEXT S
```

```
380 FOR S = 1 TO 3
390 IF T(S) = 2 THEN LET T(S) = 0
400 LET T(0) = T(0) + T(S)
410 NEXT S
420 RETURN
500 GO SUB 200
510 PRINT "ENTER ROW AND HOW MANY"
520 INPUT Y
530 IF Y = 0 THEN GO TO 900
540 IF Y < 0 OR Y > 33 THEN GO TO 520
550 LET M = Y / 10
560 LET Y = Y - 10 * M
570 IF Y > N(M) THEN GO TO 520
580 LET N(M) = N(M) - Y
590 CLS
600 GO SUB 200
610 FOR R = 1 TO 3
620 LET X(R) = N(R)
630 NEXT R
640 GO SUB 300
650 IF T(0) = 0 THEN GO TO 670
660 PRINT "I BET I WILL WIN"
670 PRINT "PRESS N/L"
680 INPUT X$
690 IF T(0) > 0 THEN GO TO 750
```

```
700 FOR R = 1 TO 3
710 LET M = N(R) - 1
720 IF N(R) > 0 THEN GO TO 820
730 NEXT R
740 GO TO 900
750 FOR R = 1 TO 3
760 FOR M = 0 TO N(R)
770 LET X(R) = M
780 GO SUB 300
790 IF T(0) = 0 THEN GO TO 820
800 NEXT M
810 NEXT R
820 IF R > 3 THEN GO TO 900
830 LET N(R) = M
840 IF N(1) + N(2) + N(3) = 0 THEN GO TO 900
850 GO TO 500
900 PRINT "WHO WON?"
```

Blackjack

This is the first of several card games in this book.

Each one uses a different approach to storing and shuffling the cards. The method used in this program is to store all 52 cards in a REM statement at the beginning of the program.

(Please note that T is used to represent 10, as this enables a single letter to be used.)

Lines 310 - 360 are used to 'shuffle' the pack by exchanging the nth card with a randomly selected one. After each game you will be able to see the shuffled pack in line 100 !

This method has the advantage of being compact and knowing that the distribution of cards is not skewed.

This program is very full, and although the computer keeps track of the total in each player's hand, there is not enough room to display this total.

Nonetheless, it still works very well within 1K, and should provide many hours of entertainment.

For those with additional memory, the following lines will display the total in each hand:

   280   PRINT "TOTAL:"
   290   PRINT N(2),,N(3)

The comments have been kept terse for the same reason, and additional memory could make the program friendlier.

Variables: N(0),N(1)   No. of cards
           N(2),N(3)   Value of hand
           A   No. of aces
           M   Money
           B   Bet
           W   Win/lose factor

Program description:
    150 - 180   Calculates value of hand
    200 - 300   Print routine
    310 - 360   Shuffling
    630 - 650   Value of aces held if over 21

Blackjack

```
100 REM 23456789TJQKA23456789TJQKA23456789
    TJQKA23456789TJQKA
110 DIM N(3)
120 LET S = 16427
130 LET M = 100
140 GO TO 310
150 LET X = PEEK (S + 6 * I + N(I)) - 28
160 LET N(I + 2) = N(I + 2) - 10 * (X > 10)
    - X * (X < 10) - 11 * (X = 10)
170 LET A = A - (X = 10)
180 RETURN
200 PRINT "YOURS",,"ZX80"
210 FOR K = 0 TO 1
220 FOR L = 6 * K TO 6 * K + N(K)
230 LET X = PEEK (S + L)
240 PRINT CHR$ (X);" ";
250 NEXT L
260 PRINT ,,
270 NEXT K
300 RETURN
310 FOR I = 0 TO 51
320 LET J = RND (52) - 1
330 LET X = PEEK (S + J)
340 POKE S + J, PEEK (S + I)
```

```
350 POKE S + I, X
360 NEXT I
370 FOR I = 0 TO 1
380 LET N(I) = 0
390 LET N(I + 2) = 0
400 LET A = 0
410 GO SUB 150
420 NEXT I
430 PRINT "BET: YOU HAVE £";M
440 INPUT B
450 CLS
500 FOR I = 0 TO 1
510 LET W = 2 * I - 1
520 LET A = N(I + 2) / 10
530 GO SUB 200
540 IF I = 0 THEN PRINT "H OR S?"
550 IF I = 1 THEN PRINT "N/L"
560 LET I$ = "S"
570 INPUT I$
580 CLS
590 IF CODE (I$) = 56 THEN GO TO 700
600 LET N(I) = N(I) + 1
610 GO SUB 150
620 IF N(I + 2) < 22 THEN GO TO 660
630 IF A = 0 THEN GO TO 800
```

```
640 LET A = A - 1
650 LET N(I + 2) = N(I + 2) - 10
660 IF N(I) = 4 THEN GO TO 700
670 IF I = 0 OR N(I + 2) < 17 THEN GO TO
    530
700 NEXT I
750 GO SUB 200
760 LET W = - 1
770 IF (N(0) = 4 AND N(1) < 4) OR N(2) >
    N(3) THEN LET W = 1
780 IF N(2) = 21 AND N(0) = 1 THEN LET W
    = 2
800 LET M = M + W * B
810 IF M < 1 THEN STOP
820 GO TO 310
```

Bubble Sort

This is a useful subroutine, more than
a program, to order the elements in an array

It assumes that there has been previously
defined an array P(I), with N elements.

The method is called a Bubble Sort
because the lighter elements 'bubble' up
to the top until each element is in its
place.

For an example of this subroutine in
a program, see BRIDGE BIDDING.

Bubble sort

```
100 FOR J = 1 TO N - 1
110 LET K = J + 1
120 FOR I = K TO N
130 LET L = N + K - 1
140 IF P(L) > P(J) THEN GO TO 180
150 LET T = P(L)
160 LET P(L) = P(J)
170 LET P(J) = T
180 NEXT I
190 NEXT J
```

Line Renumber

This is a useful routine to have, even though in its short form it takes up just over 100 bytes.

Although it can be keyed in at any time, this is tedious and it is better to LOAD it into the memory before you key in any other program. Please note that you cannot LOAD it from tape once you already have a program in the memory.

The program assumes that the first program line is already numbered 100 and will not renumber it.

Lines 9991 and 9992 tell you where GO SUBs and GO TOs are, but does not alter them. (This would not be possible with the versatile system the ZX 80 uses, in any case).

These lines can easily be deleted if short of memory.

Line Renumber

```
9989 LET L = 110
9990 FOR N = 16425 TO 17400
9993 IF NOT PEEK (N) = 118 THEN GO TO 9999
9994 IF PEEK (N + 1) > 38 THEN STOP
9995 PRINT 256 * PEEK (N + 1) + PEEK (N + 2),
9996 PRINT L
9997 LET N = N + 2
9998 LET L = L + 10
9999 NEXT N
```

>R*U*N 9989 TO SEE THAT THE PROGRAM HAS BEEN ENTERED CORRECTLY.
SCREEN SHOULD SHOW OLD LINE NUMBER AND REPLACEMENT LINE NUMBER

```
9991 IF PEEK (N) = 251 THEN PRINT L - 10,
     CHR$ (251)
9992 IF PEEK (N) = 236 THEN PRINT L - 10,
     CHR$ (236)
9995 POKE N + 1, L / 256
9996 POKE N + 2, L AND 255
```

Draw A Picture

This program will not teach you how to be a Van Gogh, but should let you play with shapes and the graphics characters so that your programs can benefit from better visual displays.

The next two pages illustrate some of the graphics characters with their code numbers.

Enter code 0 at any location to 'rub it out'.

Enter 0 as the coordinate to finish.

Available from the keyboard:

2 ▮▯ 3 ▯▮(bottom)

4 ▛ 5 ▜

6 ▙ 7 ▟

8 (checker) 9 (hatched)

10 (bottom hatched) 11 (top hatched)

Not available from the keyboard:

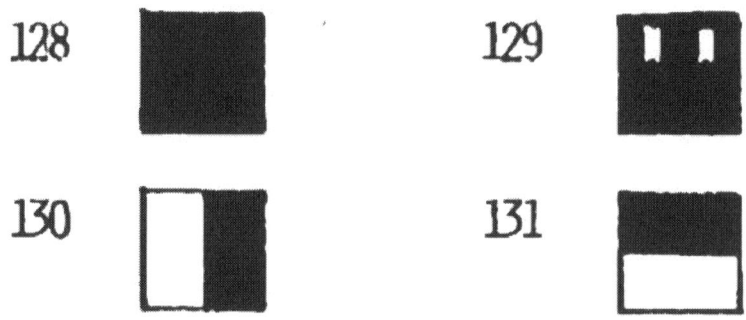

128 (solid black)   129 (black with two small white notches)

130 (white left, black right)   131 (black top, white bottom)

132    133

134    135

136    142

Other useful 'graphic' symbols:

6   £   18   -   19   +

20   *   23   >   24   <

Draw A Picture

```
100 PRINT
110 PRINT
120 PRINT "SIZE PAD (3-7)?"
130 INPUT N
140 IF N < 3 OR N > 7 THEN GO TO 120
150 DIM A(N * N - 1)
200 CLS
210 FOR K = 1 TO N
220 LET J = N + 1 - K
230 PRINT J,
240 FOR I = 1 TO N
250 PRINT CHR$ (A(J - N - 1 + N * I));
260 NEXT I
270 PRINT
280 NEXT K
290 PRINT
300 PRINT ,
310 FOR I = 1 TO N
320 PRINT I;
330 NEXT I
340 PRINT
400 PRINT "ENTER COORD"
410 INPUT X
420 IF X = 0 THEN GO TO 500
```

```
430 PRINT X
440 LET J = X / 10
450 LET I = X - 10 * J
460 PRINT "ENTER CHAR CODE"
470 INPUT X
480 LET A(J - N - 1 + N * I) = X
490 GO TO 200
500 PRINT "CODES USED:"
510 FOR K = 1 TO N
520 LET J = N + 1 - K
530 PRINT "LINE:";J,
540 FOR I = 1 TO N
550 PRINT A(J - N - 1 + N * I);" ";
560 NEXT I
570 PRINT
580 NEXT K
```

Machine Code

This program defines a reserved area of 20 bytes by defining the variable A(10) as the very first statement of the program, and then allows you to load machine code instructions in hexadecimal.

The scope of this book does not allow a full discussion of the ZX 80 machine code and how to program in machine code. A full discussion and sample programs is contained in our book **ZX 80 Machine Language Programming**.

A sample program which may prove useful is given here:

```
OR A            B7
LD HL,(16400)   2A 10 40
SBC HL, SP      ED 72
RET             C9
```

The first line (OR A) is for internal housekeeping and clears the carry flag.

The next line (LD HL,(16400)) loads the
HL counter - 16 bits - with the contents
of memory locations 16400 and 16401.
2A is the general instruction and the next
two bytes define the location 16400. Note
that it is least significant byte first.

SBC HL,SP subtracts the contents of SP
from the contents of HL.

Finally as with all subroutines, RET
is the return from the USR call.

As locations 16400 and 16401 contain the
address of the end of the visual display and
SP is the address of the stack pointer,
the difference is the amount of memory left.

This machine code routine can be used
within a program, to prevent the system
crashing - eg IF USR(S) < 20 THEN GO TO ..

Machine Code

```
100 DIM A(10)
110 LET S = PEEK (16392) + 256 * PEEK (16393) + 2
120 CLS
130 PRINT "LOCATION","CONTENTS"
140 FOR I = 0 TO 20
150 PRINT S + I,,
160 INPUT A$
170 IF A$ = "" THEN GO TO 200
180 LET V = 16 * CODE (A$) + CODE (TL$ (A$)) - 476
190 POKE S + I, V
200 LET V = PEEK (S + I)
210 PRINT CHR$(V / 16 + 28);CHR$((V AND 15) + 28)
220 IF V = 201 THEN GO TO 240
230 NEXT I
240 PRINT
250 PRINT "ANY CHANGES?"
260 INPUT A$
270 IF CODE (A$) = 62 THEN GO TO 120
280 PRINT "RESULT OF USR IS";USR(S)
```

> R*U*N
ENTER FOLLOWING MACHINE CODE VALUES
B7, 2A, 10, 40, ED, 72, C9

RESULT OF USR WILL BE - MEMORY REMAINING.
YOU MAY FIND IT INTERESTING TO ADD THE
FOLLOWING FOUR LINES:

290 PRINT "CONTENTS OF A(I) ARE:"
300 FOR I = 0 TO 3
310 PRINT A(I),
320 NEXT I

MEMORY LEFT

For those of you who worked through the previous program, you will have realised that a machine code program was stored in an ordinary variable A, and that the machine code was exactly the same as the variable A storing numbers!

This means that if you know the right numbers you can have a machine code routine without the hexadecimal coding, etc.

After you have RUN the 8 line program, most of the information is stored in the memory and you can delete 5 of those lines!

If you are desperately short of memory you can also delete line 80: Use GO TO 30, then enter on the edit line PRINT USR(S). The correct value of S will still be in memory.

Memory Left

```
20 DIM A(3)
30 LET S = PEEK (16392) + 256 * PEEK (16393) + 2
40 LET A(0) = 10935
50 LET A(1) = 16400
60 LET A(2) = 29421
70 LET A(3) = 201
80 PRINT USR(S)
90 STOP
```

> R*U*N

AFTER THE FIRST RUN, AS LONG AS YOU DO NOT CLEAR OR RUN THEN LINES 20,40,50,60 AND 70 CAN BE DELETED.

TO OBTAIN MEMORY LEFT AFTER THESE LINES HAVE BEEN DELETED USE G*O T*O 30.

Day of the Week

The computer shows off!

Give it your birth date, and the computer will tell you the day of the week when you were born.

As long as you don't strain its credulity too much (the ZX 80 finds it difficult to believe that there are people who are over 280 years old!), it will do it again and again.

Day of the Week

```
100 PRINT "   I CALCULATE THE DAY YOU WERE BORN"
110 LET D$ = "   SUNMONTUEWEDTHUFRISAT"
120 PRINT "PLEASE ENTER YOUR NAME"
130 INPUT A$
140 PRINT "HELLO ";A$
150 PRINT "ENTER DATE OF BIRTH: DAY",
160 INPUT D
170 IF D < 1 OR D > 31 THEN GO TO 160
180 PRINT D,"MONTH",
190 INPUT M
200 PRINT M,"YEAR"
210 INPUT Y
220 IF Y < 1700 THEN PRINT A$," IS TOO OLD FOR ME"
230 IF Y < 1700 THEN GO TO 440
240 CLS
250 LET K = 0
260 IF M = 1 OR M = 2 THEN LET K = 1
270 LET L = Y - K
280 LET O = M + 12 * K
290 LET P = L / 100
300 LET Z = (13 * (O + 1)) / 5 + (5 * L)
    / 4 - P + P / 4 + D - 1
```

```
310 LET Z = Z - 7 * (Z / 7) + 1
320 FOR I = 1 TO Z * 3
330 LET D$ = TL$ (D$)
340 NEXT I
400 PRINT A$;" WAS BORN ON ";CHR$( CODE (
    D$));
410 LET D$ = TL$ (D$))
420 PRINT CHR$ (CODE (D$));CHR$ (CODE ( TL$
    (D$)))
440 PRINT "ANYONE ELSE?"
450 INPUT A$
460 IF CODE (A$) = 62 THEN GO TO 110
470 PRINT "ZX80 SAYS BYEBYE"
```

Chinese Remainder

The computer as mind reader!

Every computer has one of these, and the ZX 80 is no exception.

Think of a number, divide by 5, tell me the remainder, divide the original number by 7, tell me the remainder, divide your original number by 9 and tell me the remainder - I'll let the ZX 80 tell you what number you thought of.

Chinese Remainder

```
100 DIM R(3)
110 PRINT "THINK OF A NUMBER BETWEEN 1 AND 316"
120 PRINT "PRESS N/L WHEN READY"
130 INPUT A$
200 LET A = 3
210 FOR I = 1 TO 3
220 LET A = A + 2
230 PRINT "NOW DIVIDE YOUR ORIGINAL NUMBER BY ";A
240 PRINT "PLEASE ENTER REMAINDER"
250 INPUT R(I)
260 PRINT R(I)
270 NEXT I
300 LET A = 126 * R(1) + 225 * R(2) + 280 * R(3)
310 LET A = A - 315 * (A / 315)
320 PRINT "YOUR NUMBER WAS ";A
330 PRINT "ANOTHER?"
340 INPUT A$
350 CLS
360 IF CODE (A$) = 62 THEN GO TO 100
370 PRINT "BYEBYE"
```

SIMPLE SIMON

This is the game of Simple Simon with some nice graphics touches only the ZX 80 is capable of easily.

The computer generates a random sequence of letters that you have to copy.

The nice part is that the letters are displayed in HUGE 7-line deep graphics. The key to this is that the code which defines each letter for the ZX 80 can be peeked in ROM at location 3584 onwards. Each letter is made up of 64 dots and it takes 8 bytes to define each letter.

Lines 230 - 300 PEEK and extract the 64 pieces of information.

Simple Simon

```
100 DIM A(30)
110 LET J = -1
120 RANDOMISE
130 DIM P(7)
140 FOR I = 0 TO 7
150 LET P(I) = 2 ** (7 - I)
160 NEXT I
200 LET X = RND (26) + 37
210 CLS
220 PRINT "NEXT CHAR IS"
230 FOR L = 0 TO 7
240 LET V = PEEK (3584 + L + 8 * X)
250 FOR K = 0 TO 7
260 LET G = (V AND P(K)) > 0
270 PRINT CHR$ (-128 * G);
280 NEXT K
290 PRINT
300 NEXT L
400 IF X = 15 THEN GO TO 700
410 LET J = J + 1
420 IF J = 31 THEN GO TO 800
430 LET A(J) = X
440 PRINT "PRINT ENTIRE SEQUENCE"
450 INPUT A$
```

```
460 PRINT A$
470 FOR I = 0 TO J
480 LET X = CODE (A$)
490 IF NOT A(I) = X THEN GO TO 600
500 LET A$ = TL$ (A$)
510 NEXT I
520 GO TO 200
600 LET X = 15
610 GO TO 230
700 PRINT "SORRY IT WAS:"
710 FOR I = 0 TO J
720 PRINT CHR$ (A(I));
730 NEXT I
740 STOP
800 PRINT "I GIVE UP"
```

Hangman

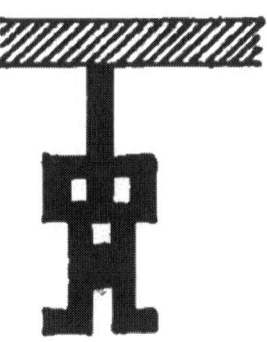

This is a 2 or more player game: one person thinks of a secret word and the other has to guess the letters that make up the word.

After 10 wrong letter guesses, this nice person here is hung, and the game is finished.

Important note: as the beginning of the program is used to define the graphics shape, use RUN 300 to run this program.

HANGMAN

```
10 PRINT "███";
20 RETURN
30 PRINT "███"
40 RETURN
50 PRINT "   ▯"
60 RETURN
70 PRINT "   ▯"
80 RETURN
90 PRINT "  "; CHR$ (135); CHR$ (135); "▯"
100 RETURN
110 PRINT "  "; CHR$ (134);
120 RETURN
130 PRINT CHR$ (134); "▯"
140 RETURN
150 PRINT "  "; CHR$ (130); CHR$ (128)
160 RETURN
170 PRINT "  "; CHR$ (132);
180 RETURN
190 PRINT CHR$ (130); "▯"
200 RETURN
210 FOR L = 1 TO G
220 IF G = 0 THEN GO TO 250
230 GO SUB 20 * L - 10
```

```
240 NEXT L
250 PRINT
260 PRINT
270 IF G = 10 THEN GO TO 290
280 GO TO 500
290 PRINT "TOO BAD"
300 PRINT "ENTER NEW WORD"
310 INPUT X$
320 LET W = 1
330 LET A$ = X$
340 FOR L = 1 TO 20
350 LET A$ = TL$ (A$)
360 IF A$ = "" THEN GO TO 390
370 LET W = W + 1
380 NEXT L
390 DIM A(W)
400 FOR L = 1 TO W
410 LET A(L) = 0
420 NEXT L
430 PRINT "LETTERS=";W
440 LET G = 0
500 PRINT "INPUT GUESS"
510 INPUT A$
520 CLS
530 IF A$ = "" THEN GO TO 999
```

```
540 LET B = CODE (A$)
550 LET A$ = X$
560 LET C = 0
570 FOR L = 1 TO W
580 IF B = CODE (A$) THEN LET A(L) = B
590 IF A(L) = B THEN LET C = 1
600 LET A$ = TL$ (A$)
610 NEXT L
620 IF C = 0 THEN LET G = G + 1
630 LET N = W
640 FOR L = 1 TO W
650 IF A(L) = 0 THEN PRINT "-";
660 IF A(L) = 0 THEN GO TO 690
670 LET N = N - 1
680 PRINT CHR$ (A(L));
690 NEXT L
700 PRINT
710 PRINT
720 IF NOT N = 0 THEN GO TO 210
730 PRINT "BRILLIANT"
740 GO TO 300
999 PRINT "THANKS FOR THE GAME"
```

Important note:

To run this program, use R*U*N 3*0*0.

Maths Drill

This program is designed to encourage the use of Computer Aided Learning for younger children.

The test itself is pretty basic - two numbers between 1 and 49 are randomly chosen and half the time you have to add them and the other half subtract them.

The encouragement comes from the oversized display of the numbers - see the notes accompanying SIMPLE SIMON for program details.

Because the oversized display uses so much memory, the program is very full, and consequently not as conversational as one might have liked.

Maths Drill

```
100 RANDOMISE
110 DIM c(3)
120 DIM p(7)
130 FOR J = 0 TO 7
140 LET p(J) = 2 ** (7 - J)
150 NEXT J
160 GO TO 400
200 IF s = -1 THEN LET c(1) = 18
210 LET c(2) = x / 10
220 LET c(3) = x - 10 * c(2) + 28
230 IF c(2) > 0 THEN LET c(2) = c(2) + 28
240 FOR L = 0 TO 6
250 FOR I = 1 TO 3
260 LET v = PEEK (3584 + L + 8 * c(I))
270 FOR J = 0 TO 7
280 LET G = (v AND p(J)) > 0
290 PRINT CHR$ (-128 * G);
300 NEXT J
310 NEXT I
320 PRINT
330 NEXT L
340 PRINT
350 RETURN
400 LET K = 0
```

```
410 LET c(1) = 0
420 LET S = 1
430 LET A = RND (49)
440 LET X = A
450 GO SUB 200
460 LET c(1) = 19
470 LET S = 2 * RND (2) - 3
480 LET B = RND (49)
490 LET X = B
500 GO SUB 200
600 INPUT C
610 IF C = A + S * B THEN GO TO 700
620 LET K = K + 1
630 IF K > 2 THEN GO TO 660
640 PRINT "TRY AGAIN"
650 GO TO 600
660 PRINT "THE ANSWER WAS "; A + S * B
670 STOP
700 PRINT "THAT/S RIGHT"
```

CAPITALS OF THE WORLD

This program illustrates another aspect of Computer Aided Learning.

Ten questions are selected in a random order - in this case world capitals - and the answers scored.

Note that both the question and answer are stored in the one variable A$, and therefore very little has to be kept in memory.

The program format is adaptable to any subject, from French vocabulary to the chemical table of elements.

CAPITALS OF THE WORLD

```
100 DIM Q(10)
110 LET C = 0
120 LET Q = 0
130 PRINT "THIS IS A TEST OF CAPITALS"
140 PRINT "WHAT IS THE CAPITAL OF."
150 LET X = RND (10)
160 LET A = 10
170 IF Q(X) < 0 THEN GO TO 150
180 LET Q(X) = - 1
190 GO SUB 500 + 20 * X
200 FOR I = 1 TO 30
210 LET X = CODE (A$)
220 PRINT CHR$ (X);
230 LET A$ = TL$ (A$)
240 IF X = 15 THEN GO TO 300
250 NEXT I
300 INPUT B$
310 IF NOT A$ = B$ THEN GO TO 400
320 LET C = C + A
330 LET Q = Q + 1
340 IF Q = 10 THEN GO TO 500
350 IF A = 0 THEN GO TO 140
360 CLS
370 GO TO 140
```

```
400 PRINT "TRY AGAIN"
410 INPUT B$
420 LET A = 5
430 IF B$ = A$ THEN GO TO 320
440 PRINT "IT IS ";A$
450 LET A = 0
460 GO TO 320
500 PRINT "YOU GOT ";C;" PERCENT RIGHT"
520 LET A$ = "CZECHOSLOVAKIA?PRAGUE"
530 RETURN
540 LET A$ = "TURKEY?ISTANBUL"
550 RETURN
560 LET A$ = "THE USA?WASHINGTON"
570 RETURN
580 LET A$ = "HOLLAND?AMSTERDAM"
590 RETURN
600 LET A$ = "AUSTRALIA?CANBERRA"
610 RETURN
620 LET A$ = "JAPAN?TOKYO"
630 RETURN
640 LET A$ = "INDIA?NEW DEHLI"
650 RETURN
660 LET A$ = "POLAND?WARSAW"
670 RETURN
680 LET A$ = "SWEDEN?STOCKHOLM"
```

690 RETURN
700 LET A$ = "PORTUGAL?LISBON"
710 RETURN

LIFE

This is a very small and necessarily limited version of the famous LIFE program, but despite its limitations it is still very interesting.

The program simulates a culture – the survival of each cell is dependent on how many neighbours it has.

Too many neighbours would imply a lack of food and the cell dies; too few neighbours and the cell is unable to reproduce or obtain support.

The rules are that a new cell is born if a space has exactly 3 neighbours, and existing cells die unless they have only 2 or 3 neighbours.

The initial population is randomly generated. The program is quite slow, so please be patient.

LIFE

```
100 DIM A(63)
110 FOR I = 1 TO 63
120 LET A(I) = 128 * (RND (2) - 1)
130 NEXT I
200 FOR L = 0 TO 8
210 FOR J = 1 TO 7
220 LET I = J + 7 * L
230 PRINT CHR$ (A(I));
240 NEXT J
250 PRINT
260 NEXT L
270 PRINT "PRESS 1"
280 INPUT A
290 CLS
300 FOR I = 9 TO 55
310 LET X = 0
320 IF ((I + 1) AND 7) = 0 THEN GO TO 350
330 LET X = (A(I + 1) > 127)
340 IF ((I - 1) AND 7) = 0 THEN GO TO 360
350 LET X = X + (A(I - 1) > 127)
360 FOR J = 7 TO 9
370 FOR R = - 1 TO 1
380 IF R = 0 THEN GO TO 420
390 LET K = I + R * J
```

```
400 IF (K AND 7) = 0 THEN GO TO 420
410 LET X = X + (A(K) > 127)
420 NEXT R
430 NEXT J
440 LET A(I) = A(I) - X
450 NEXT I
460 FOR I = 9 TO 55
470 IF A(I) = 3 OR A(I) = 130 OR A(I) = 131
    THEN GO TO 500
480 LET A(I) = 0
490 GO TO 510
500 LET A(I) = 128
510 NEXT I
520 GO TO 200
```

Prime Numbers

The program generates all the prime numbers from 2 to 300.

Line 150 might appear odd as it eliminates the search for a prime beyond the square root of X - this is because if a larger prime exists, the smaller factor would already have been found.

Despite this fairly limited search, the program takes quite a while.

Prime Numbers

```
100 DIM A(75)
110 LET R = 1
120 LET A(1) = 2
130 FOR X = 3 TO 300
140 FOR Y = 1 TO R
150 IF X / A(R) > A(R) THEN GO TO 180
160 IF X = (X / A(Y)) * A(Y) THEN GO TO 210
170 NEXT Y
180 LET R = R + 1
190 LET A(R) = X
200 PRINT X,
210 LET X = X + 1
220 NEXT X
```

SIMULTANEOUS EQUATIONS

This program solves simultaneous linear equations of the type

$ax + by + c = 0$
$dx + ey + f = 0$

The nice thing about working with integer arithmetic is that all solutions are either integer or integer fractions.

Lines 500 - 550 calculate the Greatest Common Denominator of any two numbers.

Variables: X(I) Equation constants
A(I) Solutions
D   Determinant
GCD   Greatest Common Denominator

Simultaneous Equations

```
100 DIM X(6)
110 DIM A(2)
120 PRINT "SOLUTIONS TO 2 EQUATIONS:"
130 PRINT "A * X + B * Y + C = 0"
140 PRINT
150 PRINT "ENTER DATA"
160 FOR I = 1 TO 6
170 PRINT CHR$ (37 + I - ((I - 1) / 3) * 3),
180 INPUT X(I)
190 PRINT X(I)
200 NEXT I
300 LET D = X(1) * X(5) - X(2) * X(4)
310 IF D = 0 THEN GO TO 900
320 LET A(1) = X(3) * X(5) - X(2) * X(6)
330 LET A(2) = - X(3) * X(4) + X(1) * X(6)
340 PRINT
350 PRINT "SOLUTIONS ARE"
360 LET D = - D
370 LET S = D / ABS (D)
400 FOR I = 1 TO 2
410 LET B = ABS (D)
420 LET A = ABS (A(I))
500 LET Q = A / B
510 LET R = A - Q * B
```

```
520 LET A = B
530 LET B = R
540 IF R > 0 THEN GO TO 500
550 LET GCD = A
600 PRINT S * A(I) / GCD ;
610 IF NOT D / GCD = S THEN PRINT "/";
    ABS (D / GCD)
620 PRINT ,
630 NEXT I
640 STOP
900 PRINT "- DEGENERATE: NO SOLUTIONS"
```

Square Root
To 3 Decimal Places

This program calculates the square root of any number to three decimal places.

Note the very simple iteration used in lines 200 - 240: it may be less efficient that the iterations given in texts, but it is sufficient and overcomes the major problem with the ZX 80 - overflow.

The program also illustrates the use of variable names to make a listing more legible.

Square Root

```
100 PRINT "INPUT NUMBER"
110 INPUT A
120 CLS
130 PRINT "SQUARE ROOT OF ";A;" IS"
140 LET U = 174
150 LET L = 0
160 LET FRAC = 0
170 LET DELTA = 0
200 LET NEW = (U + L) / 2
210 IF (NEW - 1) ** 2 < A AND (NEW + 1) ** 2 > A THEN GO TO 250
220 IF NEW ** 2 > A THEN LET U = NEW
230 IF NEW ** 2 < A THEN LET L = NEW
240 GO TO 200
250 IF NEW ** 2 > A THEN LET NEW = NEW - 1
300 LET ERROR = 100 * (A - NEW ** 2)
310 IF ERROR < 2 THEN GO TO 470
320 LET FRAC = (ERROR / NEW) / 2
330 LET FSQ = FRAC ** 2
340 LET ERROR = ERROR - 2 * NEW * FRAC
350 IF ERROR > 0 THEN GO TO 390
360 LET FRAC = FRAC - 1
370 LET ERROR = 100 * (A - NEW ** 2)
380 GO TO 330
```

```
390 LET ERROR = 10 * ERROR - FSQ / 10
400 IF ERROR < 0 THEN GO TO 360
410 LET DELTA = (ERROR / NEW) / 2
420 LET EDASH = ERROR - (2 * FRAC * DELTA)
    / 2
430 IF EDASH > 0 THEN GO TO 460
440 LET DELTA = DELTA - 1
450 GO TO 420
460 LET DELTA = (EDASH / NEW) / 2
470 PRINT NEW;".";FRAC;DELTA
```

Bridge Bidding

This program will deal you a Bridge hand and asks what you would bid as an opening bid with this hand. Obviously the limitations of 1K do not allow the program to go very far, but it is still very interesting.

The cards are shuffled and dealt in the one operation (lines 120 - 170): one of 52 cards is chosen at random and each fourth card is given to the player.

A Bubble sort subroutine is used to order the 13 cards in the player's hand and it is displayed in suits.

A simple algorithm is used to calculate the points value.

Bridge Bidding

```
100 DIM D(51)
110 DIM P(13)
120 FOR I = 1 TO 52
130 LET C = RND (52) - 1
140 IF D(C) < 0 THEN GO TO 130
150 IF I = 4 * (I / 4) THEN LET P(I / 4) = C
160 LET D(C) = - 1
170 NEXT I
200 FOR J = 1 TO 12
210 LET K = J + 1
220 FOR I = K TO 13
230 LET L = 13 + K - I
240 IF P(L) > P(J) THEN GO TO 280
250 LET T = P(L)
260 LET P(L) = P(J)
270 LET P(J) = T
280 NEXT I
290 NEXT J
300 LET V = 0
310 LET C = - 1
320 FOR I = 1 TO 13
330 LET S = P(I) / 13
340 LET P(I) = P(I) - 13 * S
```

```
350 IF S = C THEN LET M = M + 1
360 IF S > C + 1 THEN LET V = V + 3
370 IF S > C THEN LET M = 0
380 IF M > 0 THEN GO TO 500
390 LET C = S
400 LET A$ = " CDHS"
410 PRINT
420 FOR J = 1 TO S + 1
430 LET A$ = TL$ (A$)
440 NEXT J
450 PRINT CHR$ ( CODE (A$));"..";
460 LET V = V + 3
500 IF P(I) > 8 THEN GO TO 530
510 PRINT P(I) + 2;" ";
520 GO TO 600
530 LET P(I) = P(I) - 8
540 LET A$ = " JQKA"
550 FOR J = 1 TO P(I)
560 LET A$ = TL$ (A$)
570 NEXT J
580 PRINT CHR$ (CODE (A$));".";
590 LET V = V + P(I)
600 IF M < 3 THEN LET V = V - 1
610 IF 10 * M > T THEN LET T = 10 * M + S
620 NEXT I
```

```
630 PRINT
640 PRINT
700 PRINT "BID?"
710 INPUT A$
720 PRINT A$
730 PRINT
740 PRINT "WE SUGGEST.";
750 IF V < 13 THEN PRINT "PASS"
760 IF V < 13 THEN GO TO 800
770 IF V < 21 THEN PRINT "1";
780 IF V > 20 THEN PRINT "2";
790 PRINT " IN LONGEST SUIT"
```

PONTOON

This is the 2 player version of BLACKJACK, with some nice card display graphics.

The program deals the cards, generated from a random number. This is equivalent to playing with a very large number of packs and the cards that fall do not have any influence on the distribution of the remaining cards.

Note the possible expansion with additional memory to display both players' cards at the same time.

Pontoon

```
100 DIM N(2)
110 DIM V(9)
120 RANDOMISE
130 FOR I = 1 TO 2
140 LET N(I) = 1
150 LET V(5 * I - 5) = RND (13)
160 NEXT I
170 LET I = 1
200 LET P = I
210 FOR L = 1 TO 7
220 FOR C = 1 TO N(P)
230 LET J = C - 6 + 5 * P
240 IF L = 1 OR L = 7 THEN GO TO 420
250 IF L = 4 THEN GO TO 270
260 GO TO 440
270 PRINT " ▨ ";
280 IF V(J) < 2 OR V(J) > 10 THEN GO TO 330
290 PRINT V(J);
300 IF V(J) < 10 THEN PRINT " ";
310 PRINT "▨";
320 GO TO 450
330 LET A$ = " AJQK"
340 LET M = V(J)
350 IF M > 10 THEN LET M = M - 9
```

```
360 FOR K = 1 TO M - 1
370 LET A$ = TL$ (A$)
380 NEXT K
390 PRINT CHR$ ( CODE (A$));
400 PRINT " ▨";
410 GO TO 450
420 PRINT " ▨▨▨▨";
430 GO TO 450
440 PRINT " ▨   ▨";
450 NEXT C
460 PRINT
470 NEXT L
480 PRINT
490 PRINT
600 PRINT "PLAYER:";I;"-HIT OR STAY?"
610 INPUT A$
620 CLS
630 IF CODE (A$) = 56 THEN GO TO 670
640 LET N(I) = N(I) + 1
650 LET V(N(I) - 6 + 5 * I) = RND (13)
660 GO TO 200
670 IF I = 2 THEN STOP
680 LET I = I + 1
690 GO TO 200
```

NOTE:

IN THE 1K VERSION, THERE IS INSUFFICIENT MEMORY TO DISPLAY BOTH THE PLAYERS' CARDS AT THE SAME TIME.

IF YOU HAVE ADDITIONAL MEMORY THEN REPLACE LINE 200 WITH
200 FOR P = 1 TO 2
AND ADD THE FOLLOWING LINE:
500 NEXT P
AS WELL, LINE 620 (CLS) SHOULD BE RENUMBERED 645.

Chomp

This is a game for 2 or more players. The game first appeared in Scientific American in January 1973.

The object is for each player to take a 'bite' out of a grid, knowing that the last bite is poisoned.

The strategies for 2 players are fairly simple but the fun starts when there are more players.

CHOMP

```
100 DIM A(48)
110 FOR I = 0 TO 48
120 LET A(I) = 6
130 NEXT I
140 LET A(0) = 53
150 PRINT "HOW MANY PLAYERS?"
160 INPUT N
170 LET T = 0
200 LET T = T + 1
210 FOR L = 0 TO 6
220 LET J = 7 - L
230 PRINT J,
240 FOR C = 0 TO 6
250 PRINT CHR$ ( A(C + 7 * L));
260 NEXT C
270 PRINT
280 NEXT L
290 PRINT ,
300 FOR C = 1 TO 7
310 PRINT C;
320 NEXT C
330 PRINT
340 PRINT "PLAYER:";T
410 PRINT "INPUT COORD"
```

```
420 INPUT A
430 IF A = 0 THEN GO TO 999
440 LET J = A / 10
450 LET C = A - 10 * J - 1
460 LET L = 7 - J
470 LET P = C + 7 * L
480 IF P < 0 OR P > 48 THEN GO TO 420
490 IF A(P) > 0 THEN GO TO 600
500 PRINT "EMPTY SPACE"
510 GO TO 410
600 IF P = 0 THEN GO TO 700
610 FOR J = L TO 6
620 FOR I = C TO 6
630 LET A(I + 7 * J) = 0
640 NEXT I
650 NEXT J
660 CLS
670 IF T = N THEN LET T = 0
680 GO TO 200
700 PRINT "PLAYER:";T;"-YOU LOST"
```

MASTERMIND

You choose the level of complexity you want to play at, and the computer will generate a code to match.

From 3 to 7 digits can be chosen, and the computer will assign a number to each digit. No two positions will contain the same number.

Variables: A Secret digits
           G Number of guesses
           R Number of digits rights
           C Number of positions right

MASTERMIND

```
100 PRINT "WELCOME TO MASTERMIND"
110 PRINT "ENTER NO OF DIGITS IN NUMBER (3-7)"
120 INPUT N
130 LET N = N - 1
140 DIM A(N)
200 FOR I = 0 TO N
210 LET X = RND (10) - 1
220 FOR J = 0 TO I
230 IF X = A(J) THEN GO TO 210
240 NEXT J
250 LET A(I) = X
260 NEXT I
270 LET G = 0
280 GO TO 530
300 INPUT B$
310 IF B$ = "" THEN STOP
320 CLS
330 PRINT B$
340 LET R = 0
350 LET C = 0
360 LET G = G + 1
370 FOR I = 0 TO N
380 LET X = CODE (B$) - 28
390 IF X = A(I) THEN LET C = C + 1
```

```
400 FOR J = 0 TO N
410 IF X = A(J) THEN LET R = R + 1
420 NEXT J
430 LET B$ = TL$ (B$)
440 NEXT I
450 IF C = N + 1 THEN GO TO 600
500 PRINT "NUMBERS RIGHT =";R
510 PRINT "CORRECT POSITIONS =";C
520 PRINT
530 PRINT "ENTER ";N + 1;"-FIGURE GUESS"
540 GO TO 300
600 PRINT "YOU DID IT IN ";G;" GUESSES"
```

PINCH

This is another game which first appeared in Scientific American, this time in 1980.

It is the Flatland equivalent of the Japanese game of Go. Two players take turns to place 'stones' on an 8 position board: a group of connected stones is considered to be captured if it is surrounded on both sides. A group on the edge is the easiest to capture.

```
- - X O - - - O
1 2 3 4 5 6 7 8
```

For example, it if was X to move, a move to place a stone on 7 would capture the group on 8. If it was O to move, placing a stone at 2 would capture the group at 3.

It is an interesting game with constantly varying fortunes. Once you have mastered the strategies of the 8 position board, try a 9 position board where the strategies are different.

Pinch

```
100 DIM G(9)
110 PRINT "ENTER PLAYER 1 NAME"
120 INPUT Y$
130 PRINT "PLAYER 2 NAME?"
140 INPUT Z$
150 LET A$ = Y$
160 LET B = 2
170 GO TO 600
200 LET C = G(I)
210 IF C = 0 THEN RETURN
220 FOR S = -1 TO 1
230 IF S = 0 THEN GO TO 330
240 FOR J = 1 TO 6
250 LET K = I + S * J
260 IF K = 9 OR K = 0 THEN GO TO 300
270 IF G(K) = 0 OR G(K) = C THEN GO TO 290
280 NEXT J
290 IF J = 1 OR G(K) = 0 THEN GO TO 330
300 FOR K = 1 TO J - 1
310 LET G(I + S * K) = 0
320 NEXT K
330 NEXT S
340 CLS
350 PRINT
```

```
360 PRINT "PINCH"
370 PRINT
380 PRINT
390 FOR J = 1 TO 8
400 PRINT "  "; CHR$ (6 + 3 * G(J));
410 NEXT J
420 PRINT
430 PRINT " ";
440 FOR J = 1 TO 8
450 PRINT "▨▨▨";
460 NEXT J
470 PRINT
480 PRINT
490 FOR J = 1 TO 8
500 PRINT "  ";J;
510 NEXT J
520 RETURN
600 GO SUB 340
610 PRINT
620 PRINT A$;":ENTER MOVE"
630 INPUT I$
640 LET I = CODE (I$) - 28
650 IF I = 0 THEN GO TO 999
660 IF I > 0 AND I < 9 THEN GO TO 680
670 GO TO 630
```

```
680 IF NOT G(I) = 0 THEN GO TO 630
690 LET G(I) = B
700 GO SUB 200
710 LET I = I + 1
720 IF I = 9 THEN LET I = 7
730 GO SUB 200
740 LET B = B + 1
750 IF B = 3 THEN LET B = 1
760 IF B = 2 THEN LET A$ = Y$
770 IF B = 1 THEN LET A$ = Z$
780 GO TO 610
```

Gomoku

This is the most ambitious program in this book, and uses the display on the screen as the only record of what is happening in the game!

Gomoku is a Japanese game played on a Go board (usually 19 x 19 grid). The object is to place stones very much in Noughts and Crosses fashion, but instead of looking for three in a row you must have 5 stones in a row to win.

As in noughts and crosses, the stones can be aligned horizontally, vertically or diagonally.

In this program the computer plays a defensive game more than an agressive game, but you will find it fairly difficult to win even though you start.

Line 100 is a REM statement which starts off as (shifted) A, but machine code values will be POKEd into these locations.

The operation of the ZX 80 Basic means that after certain values have been POKEd there the screen display hangs up if that line is displayed.

As long as you don't display line 100 the program functions very well. Should you accidentally press LIST or otherwise get that line displayed the only remedy I can suggest to delete line 100 (enter 100 followed by New Line). The line can then be rentered.

The USR program is extremely simple: all it does is return the value of the address of the screen display.

```
LD HL,(16396)
RET
```

The other data which is POKEd into the REM statement are coordinate increments for the search-for-neighbours routine.

Program description:

150 - 160	Subroutine which translates coordinate X to screen address.
200 - 340	Print routine for board. The program only executes this once, and it is not erased.
400 - 470	Input player's move and check to see if legal
1000 - 1060	Routine (later deleted) to POKE machine code values into USR statement
500 - 760	Routine which examines if player's move is part of a string. If it is response is to block the string.
800 - 840	If player move was not part of a string response is a random one.

```
100 REM ░░░░░░░░░░░░Gomoku░░░░░░░░░░░░
110 LET A = 16428
120 GO TO 200
150 LET K = USR (A) + 2 * (X AND 15) - 24
    * (X / 16) + 175
160 RETURN
200 FOR K = 1 TO 7
210 LET J = 8 - K
220 PRINT J,
230 FOR I = 1 TO 7
240 PRINT "▢ ";
250 NEXT I
260 PRINT
270 PRINT
280 NEXT K
290 PRINT ,
300 FOR K = 1 TO 7
310 PRINT K;" ";
320 NEXT K
330 PRINT
340 PRINT "INPUT COORDS"
```

NOTE:

BECAUSE OF THE WAY THIS PROGRAM IS

CONSTRUCTED, IT IS IMPORTANT TO HAVE THIS
SECTION OF THE PROGRAM WORKING PROPERLY
FROM THE BEGINNING.
PRESS R*U*N AND SEE THAT THE BOARD DISPLAY
IS CORRECTLY PRINTED.
WHEN WORKING PROPERLY ENTER C*L*E*A*R ON
THE EDIT LINE AND PRESS "NEW LINE".

400 INPUT X
410 IF X = 0 THEN GO TO 900
420 LET X = X + 6 * (X / 10)
430 LET X = X AND 119
440 IF X / 16 = 0 OR (X AND 7) = 0 THEN GO
    TO 400
450 GO SUB 150
460 IF PEEK (K) > 6 THEN GO TO 400
470 POKE K, 9
480 LET V = 77
1000 LET A = 16428
1010 FOR I = 0 TO 12
1020 PRINT A + I,
1030 INPUT J
1040 POKE A + I, J
1050 PRINT PEEK (A + I)
1060 NEXT I

NOTE:

PRESS G*0 T*0 1*0*0*0 AT THIS STAGE AND ENTER THE FOLLOWING VALUES TO BE POKED INTO THE REM STATEMENT:

16428	42
16429	12
16430	64
16431	201
16432	9
16433	113
16434	23
16435	1
16436	7
16437	17
16438	119
16439	16
16440	112

BECAUSE OF THE WAY THE ZX 80 BASIC OPERATES IT IS NOW NOT POSSIBLE TO HAVE A SCREEN DISPLAY WHICH INCLUDES THE REM LINE JUST POKED.

THEREFORE DO NOT PRESS LIST.

900 STOP

NOTE:

PRESS R*U*N TO SEE THAT USR FUNCTION IS OPERATING CORRECTLY. ENTERING AN X COORDINATE FROM 11 TO 77 SHOULD SEE THAT SQUARE POKED.

WHEN OPERATING CORRECTLY PRESS C*L*E*A*R AND DELETE LINES 900 AND 1000 - 1060.

500 LET J = 0
510 LET U = X
520 FOR L = A + 5 TO A + 12
530 LET I = 0
540 LET O = 0
550 IF 2 * (L / 2) < L THEN LET O = - 1
560 IF O THEN LET X = U
570 LET X = X + PEEK (L)
580 LET X = X AND 119
590 LET I = I + 1
600 IF X / 16 = 0 OR (X AND 15) = 0 THEN GO TO 650
610 GO SUB 150
620 IF PEEK (K) = 9 THEN GO TO 570

```
630 IF PEEK (K) = 12 AND O THEN GO TO 700
640 IF O THEN LET V = X
650 IF O THEN GO TO 700
660 IF I > J THEN LET J = I
670 IF NOT I = J THEN GO TO 700
680 LET W = X
690 IF NOT PEEK (K) = 6 THEN LET W = V
700 NEXT L
710 IF J < 3 THEN GO TO 800
720 IF J > 5 THEN GO TO 900
730 LET X = W
740 GO SUB 150
750 POKE K, 12
760 GO TO 400
800 LET X = 16 * RND (7) + RND (7)
810 GO SUB 150
820 IF NOT PEEK (K) = 6 THEN GO TO 800
830 POKE K, 12
840 GO TO 400
900 PRINT "WHO WON?"
```

You May Also Enjoy...

Printed in Great Britain
by Amazon

0c11c755-69d4-4bb1-ba5d-cb05d47e9886R01